DISCO
LON
DOCKLANDS

Chris Fautley

SHIRE PUBLICATIONS

Published in Great Britain in 2011 by Shire Publications Ltd,
Midland House, West Way, Botley, Oxford OX2 0PH, United Kingdom.

44-02 23rd Street, Suite 219, Long Island City, NY 11101, USA.

E-mail: shire@shirebooks.co.uk   www.shirebooks.co.uk

© 2011 Chris Fautley.

Every attempt has been made by the Publishers to secure the appropriate permissions for
materials reproduced in this book. If there has been any oversight we will be happy to
rectify the situation and a written submission should be made to the Publishers.

A CIP catalogue record for this book is available from the British Library.

Shire Discovering no. 305.   ISBN-13: 978 0 74780 845 9

Chris Fautley has asserted his right under the Copyright, Designs and Patents Act, 1988, to
be identified as the author of this book.

Designed by Myriam Bell Design, France and typeset in Garamond.

Printed in China through Worldprint Ltd.

11 12 13 14 15   10 9 8 7 6 5 4 3 2 1

COVER: Old meets new: cranes, under the watchful eyes of Canary Wharf skyscrapers,
stand guard over the entrance lock to the South Dock – now the only direct access to the
Thames from the West India Docks.

TITLE PAGE: On 6 August 1939 crowds line the shore as the RMS *Mauretania*, a former
holder of the Blue Riband awarded for the fastest transatlantic crossing in passenger service,
inches her way through the entrance lock to the King George V Dock.

ACKNOWLEDGEMENTS

Special thanks are due to all those who, through various means, have supported the
preparation of this book, and in particular: Urban Space Management; the team at Shire,
for whom nothing has ever been too much trouble; and last, but not least, the many
friends who have shown such enthusiasm and interest in the project from its inception.

Additionally, permission to use illustrations provided by the following is gratefully
acknowledged:

Getty Images, pages 37 (top), and 70; Mary Evans Picture Library, page 51; Museum of
London, pages 9, 34, 44 and 79; National Maritime Museum, Greenwich, London, page
52; Museum of London/PLA Collection, pages 9, 34, 44; Popperfoto/Getty Images,
title page; Print Collector/HIP/Topfoto, page 10.

All other illustrations are from the author's collection.

CONTENTS

INTRODUCTION

W HEN I first put forward the idea of a visitor's guide to Docklands, I had a pretty good idea what I was going to write about – or at least I thought I had. But during one of those unhelpful authorial moments of staring at a blank sheet of paper I had an equally unhelpful thought: just what, exactly, *is* Docklands? For most people (and I respectfully exclude all former dockers and East Londoners, because they know better), Canary Wharf and its tower are one of the first things that come to mind. But Canary Wharf is a mere brush stroke in the bigger picture that is Docklands. Canary Wharf covers less than 100 acres – not even 2 per cent of the area that the London Docklands Development Corporation was tasked with redeveloping.

So, then, the Royal Docks would be included, together with Silvertown – the area to the south between the Royals and the river – and the rest of the Isle of Dogs, on whose northern tip Canary Wharf stands. Maybe, I thought, I should take a look at Blackwall, an area that I knew had potential although I was less familiar with it. Then I had to consider Surrey Docks – 'Surrey Quays', as the district is now more trendily called – and the Lower and Upper Pools of London, the stretch of river roughly between Limehouse and London Bridge. Then there is St Katharine's Dock, too – and numerous other small concerns to its east. And what about all the wharves downstream; should Tilbury be included?

Opposite: Cranes line the entrance lock to the South Dock of West India Docks, while the modern skyline of Canary Wharf peers down from behind.

It soon transpired that there simply would not be sufficient space to include everything. Thus, St Katharine's Dock and most of the smaller docks have been omitted, except in passing; sadly, much of their heritage has been swept away, although St Katharine's Dock is designated a conservation area. Several of its warehouses remain – albeit as pubs, shops and restaurants. South of the river, the Surrey Docks, whose former significance should not be underestimated, have also been left out – largely because most of them (with the notable exception of Greenland Dock and Canada Water) have been infilled and redeveloped with shopping centres and housing. This is despite feeling a sense of familial duty to include them, as my mother was born within walking distance of them and my great uncle was a stevedore there.

My decision to exclude these districts was also influenced by what I found in those that are included. In many instances, I found far more than I anticipated: the East India Docks did not feature in the original synopsis, and yet I found them to be one of the most fruitful areas. Similarly, Trinity Buoy Wharf was only to have the briefest of mentions – until I investigated in greater depth.

So this book focuses on the north of the river: Canary Wharf, Blackwall, the Isle of Dogs, the Royal Docks, and Silvertown – which, it is hoped, will fall within most people's perception of 'Docklands'.

The only remaining warehouses at St Katharine's Dock, named the Ivory House, were built in 1860. These days the dock's principal function is for leisure, with some retail and residential use.

DOCKLANDS PAST AND PRESENT

L ONDON'S history as a port through which water-borne trade was conducted stretches back more than two thousand years. However, its history of trade conducted through docks – that is, enclosed bodies of water – is considerably shorter. For centuries, trade had taken place through riverside wharves; larger vessels moored midstream, their contents being ferried ashore by lighters. Because many cargoes were extremely valuable, the temptation for theft was high, and willingly succumbed to.

Small docks, consisting of fingers of water leading from the river, perhaps able to accommodate just two or three ships, had started to appear as early as the seventeenth century. However, it was not until the early nineteenth century that the need for fully warehoused and enclosed docks became urgent. As well as the added benefits of security and centralisation, the provision of locks connecting them to the river meant that trade became far less dependent on the tides.

Thus, in 1799, the West India Dock Act was passed allowing the West India Dock Company, a company founded exclusively for the purpose by a group of merchants who traded with the West Indies, to start work on enclosed docks, wharves and warehouses. The project, on the Isle of Dogs, was completed by 1806.

The idea soon caught on. A year earlier, the London Docks had opened at Wapping; within thirty years, the St Katharine's and East India docks and part of the Surrey Docks complex had all been built. Others followed later, the final significant undertaking being the King George V Dock, part of the 'Royals' group, opened in 1921.

Business flourished, and docks soon came to specialise in certain types of cargo. Greenland Dock (part of Surrey Docks), for example, initially specialised in the whaling industry, Millwall in grain, and the East India group in merchandise handled by the East India Company, and so on. The port of London became an enormous bulk storehouse, with merchandise arriving from throughout the

The tidal Limekiln Dock, near Canary Wharf, was typical of the many small docks that served east London before the advent of larger, enclosed enterprises protected from the tides by locks.

This photograph, taken in 1954, shows grain elevators at a busy-looking Royal Victoria Dock, overlooked by the now demolished Co-op flour mill.

British Empire and the world. From the outset the dock complexes, except the King George V, were independent concerns; only in 1909, with the incorporation of the Port of London Authority, did they all come under one organisation.

In the Second World War Docklands became a prime target for the Luftwaffe. The worst came during the Blitz when, from 7 September 1940, London was bombed on fifty-seven consecutive nights. Almost 20,000 tons of explosive fell on the city – a sizable proportion being targeted at the docks; it is estimated some 25,000 bombs hit Docklands during the entire war. As well as the inevitable destruction, there was also a huge amount of human suffering and damage to infrastructure. Yet somehow, the docks continued to function.

After the war there were new difficulties. Deteriorating labour relations took their toll, while London's docks were ill-equipped to

Quayside warehouses, West India Import Dock, 1927. The barrels contain molasses. The taller warehouse now houses the splendid Museum of Docklands.

cope with larger ships and the increasing popularity of containerisation. Accordingly, trade switched to ports better able to cope – such as Tilbury, downstream. Business became quieter and quieter; and the inevitable decay set in.

The East India Docks were the first to succumb, in 1967. Several more had followed suit by 1968, although the Royals, West India and Millwall Docks lasted, in a much reduced capacity, until the early 1980s. London had thus acquired a vast and unwanted wilderness of dereliction. There had been murmurings of positive action as early as the 1970s, but it was not until 1981 that a concerted effort was made with the formation of the London Docklands Development Corporation (LDDC).

Regeneration is a concept that has become firmly associated with the late twentieth and early twenty-first centuries. The brief of the LDDC, however, was to take the meaning of the word into hitherto almost unheard-of proportions: to regenerate 8½ square miles of east and south London – essentially Docklands. A principal aim was

New homes overlook the former East India Docks entrance basin, while the skyline is dominated by the towering office blocks of Canary Wharf.

to provide employment for the more than ten thousand workers who had lost their jobs with the docks' decline. Some work had already been undertaken by local authorities: London Docks, Surrey Docks and most of the East India Docks had largely been filled in. Now, any action would come under the LDDC's central umbrella. Unsurprisingly, there was not a little resentment from local people, who considered that social needs, such as housing, were often neglected in favour of grander, commercial development.

This is not the place in which to list the LDDC's achievements in vast detail. Suffice to say that during its lifetime it secured almost £10 billion worth of public and private investment. It has overseen a huge rise in employment, the construction of the Docklands Light Railway, London City Airport, thousands of new homes, and many miles of new or improved roads.

By 1998 its work was considered largely done: regeneration had been kick-started and in many instances was positively racing. Nonetheless, there is still much to do, although most of this is considered to be well within the capabilities of the various London boroughs. Such large projects as remain will fall within the auspices of English Partnerships, Britain's principal regeneration authority. Though there is still some way to go, Docklands is thriving once more.

GETTING AROUND

DOCKLANDS, fortunately for explorers, is blessed with the kind of infrastructure that other places can only envy, although occasionally it was a little late in coming.

The principal means of getting about – apart from walking – is the Docklands Light Railway (DLR), and reference is regularly made to its stations throughout this book. The service is excellent; and, as it carries some 70 million passengers a year, there are as many as fifteen trains per hour running on some routes. Much of it runs above street level, thus affording excellent views. A Zones 1–3 Travelcard is the best-value way of getting around, giving unlimited travel (subject to its terms and conditions) throughout all the districts covered in this book. London Underground's Jubilee Line, meanwhile, connects with the DLR at Canary Wharf and Canning Town. And, if you wish to arrive in style, riverboats serve Canary Wharf Pier.

Do not be misled by Transport for London's definitive map of the DLR. Like the London Underground map, it is not especially to scale, and some of the stations are incredibly close together. Little more than 200 yards separate West India Quay and Canary Wharf stations, while between Canary Wharf and Heron Quays it is even less. As a general rule, the further away from the central area of Canary Wharf, the greater the distance between stations.

Additionally, the DLR is ideal for a whistlestop tour of Docklands, should time be at a premium. To see Canary Wharf, the West India Docks and the Isle of Dogs in all their glory, take a train from Poplar to Mudchute. Alternatively, for views of the Royal

Docks, London City Airport and what remains of the East India Docks complex, take a train from Poplar to Gallions Reach.

Obviously, be prepared to walk – again, rather longer distances the further one is from the central area. Invest in a good street map: while I have done my best to provide accurate directions within the text, it is all too easy to become lost without one. And do be sure it is to a decent scale; I used one with a scale of 9 inches to the mile. Anything less and I would have struggled.

Also, be prepared for change. Docklands is an evolving area: vast swathes are still relatively undeveloped, and even amid the hubris of Canary Wharf there is still a tremendous amount of building work being undertaken. Inevitably, you will find – and probably be delighted by – things that this book does not even mention: a little hidden gem of history, or some awe-inspiring building that was not built when the book was written. Such things merely add to the pleasure of discovering London's Docklands.

One of the greatest successes in Docklands, the Docklands Light Railway, here seen near East India station, has been serving the district since 1987; it has been growing ever since – in terms of both capacity and destinations served.

THE ROYAL DOCKS

THE DOCKS of the Royal group – Royal Albert, Royal Victoria and King George V – were among the last to be built in Docklands and, in 1981, the last to close. An enormous undertaking, together they formed at one time the world's largest enclosed dock system, the water alone amounting to almost 250 acres. They were also at the forefront of technology. For example, the Victoria was one of the first docks to use hydraulic machinery. Railways were also used extensively: at its peak, the Victoria's extensive network of sidings could easily accommodate more than one thousand wagons.

The Albert and Victoria docks lie end to end, stretching a total distance of 2 miles; their combined area of water is 175 acres. A fine spot from which to appreciate their length is the west side of the bridge across the Albert Basin on Woolwich Manor Way (a very short walk south of Gallions Reach DLR station), at the docks' far eastern end. (The basin now serves as a yachting marina.) Water stretches seemingly as far as the eye can see; even the skyscrapers at Canary Wharf in the distance seemed dwarfed. To the south of the Royal Albert, and parallel to it, is the King George V Dock.

The west side of the bridge is also an excellent point from which to view the cylindrical buildings of the University of East London's Docklands campus designed by Edward Cullinan. Variously likened

Opposite: Student accommodation of the University of East London, overlooking the Royal Albert Dock. As London City Airport is just a few hundred yards across the water, the buildings have been soundproofed.

to salt and pepper cruets or oil drums, they are brightly coloured and line the northern quay of the Albert Dock. The 'cruets' are built in pairs, and in profile the roofs are reminiscent of a seagull in flight. They have few windows – to minimise noise from London City Airport, which is sited on the opposite side of the dock. It is possible to gain a closer view of these buildings by leaving the bridge and following the quayside path, or Cyprus DLR station leads immediately on to the campus.

King George V Dock

The bridge, being little more than 400 yards from the eastern end of the runway, is just one of several vantage points from which to take in the airport. Depending on the wind direction, arriving and departing aircraft seem to be within arm's reach. The runway is built on a former wharf, effectively the narrow strip of land that separated the King George V and Albert docks. The former was opened, at a cost of £4.5 million, in July 1921, its completion having been delayed by the onset of the First World War. Its water covered

Taken from the bridge on Woolwich Manor Way across the Albert Basin, this view shows the enormous length of the Royal Albert Dock and the Royal Victoria Dock beyond. The connecting channel to the King George V Dock is on the left.

64 acres, it was almost 1 mile long, and it had a dry dock, 3 miles of quayside, and the latest in electric cranes. Its principal cargoes were fruit, vegetables, frozen meat and grain.

On its south side was a series of jetties, or dolphins, upon which were mounted cranes. These ran parallel with the main quay, the two being separated by a narrow length of water that was able to accommodate barges. Accordingly, arriving vessels moored on one side of the jetties, where they were unloaded by cranes, whose reach was such that cargoes could either be discharged on to waiting barges for onward transhipment, or craned on to the adjacent wharf for storage in its warehouses. Warehouses on both north and south quays had the additional benefit of being rail-served.

Of the rail links and warehouses that served the King George V, nothing remains. The site of the dry dock is occupied by the airport apron and terminal building of London City Airport; but it has vanished, however, only in the sense that it is not visible: the dock was not infilled but, in rather more impressive fashion, boxed in with steel girders. The apron and terminal building are effectively built on an enormous raft; some indication of its size may be gained from the fact that the dry dock was well able to accommodate vessels approaching 30,000 tons.

The first commercial flight arrived in 1987, although this was not the first aircraft to land in Docklands. That had happened five years earlier and is covered in the chapter on 'Canary Wharf and Riverside'. The idea of

The threshold of London City Airport's runway, and the Canary Wharf skyline beyond. Rail-served warehouses once stood on the site of the runway.

an airport had been mooted as early as 1981; however, owing to planning difficulties, including a public enquiry, it was 1986 before construction commenced. The limited amount of space available for a runway meant that it became one of the original STOL ports (Short Take-Off and Landing); the smaller aircraft that were best suited to this type of operation were also, by good fortune, ideal for complying with the strict noise limitations that were part of the planning consent.

Operations got off to a very slow start; initially there were flights only to Paris and Brussels. Poor infrastructure was part of the problem: it was all well and good having an airport within 6 miles of the City of London, but not so helpful when the only means of reaching it was by bus or an expensive taxi ride. However, matters gradually improved, culminating in the arrival of the Docklands Light Railway in December 2005.

London City built on its shaky start, to the effect that thirty destinations throughout Britain and continental Europe are now served. Aircraft noise improvements and expansion of the runway from its initial 2,500 feet have enabled New York to be added to the list of destinations, although the runway is still not long enough to

The entrance lock to the King George V Dock; the river is beyond. The former custom house is on the left.

allow the aircraft to take off with a full load of fuel; subsequently, it has to call at Shannon en route to take on its full capacity. The airport now handles some three million passengers annually.

Viewed from Woolwich Manor Way, only a few clues remain (apart from the now tranquil stretches of water) that this district was ever a thriving port. Some of these may be found by continuing a few hundred yards along the road to the bascule bridge that crosses the entrance lock to the King George V. Like the dock, the bridge dates from the early 1920s.

As one looks west, the entire length of the dock may be seen, as well as the short connecting channel linking it with the Royal Albert. It is from the opposite side of the road, however, that most of the dock's remaining history is visible. First and foremost is the entrance lock, one of the few remaining operational locks in Docklands. In August 1939 crowds lined the lockside to watch the liner *Mauretania* passing through on its way to the King George V Dock. The width of the lock was 100 feet; that of the *Mauretania* 89 feet 6 inches. It must have been a very tight squeeze.

On the north side of the lock stands the custom house – a rather long single-storey building no longer used for its original purpose. On the opposite side, the diminutive red and black brick lock-keeper's office still oversees proceedings. Modern flats lie behind.

The Royal Albert Dock

The far larger Royal Albert Dock (DLR: Cyprus, Beckton Park or Royal Albert) lies due north of the King George V and the City Airport runway. Along with the rest of the Royals, it was built on what was marshland. Promoted by the London & St Katharine Dock Company, it opened in 1880, and it has been suggested that it was not intended to be a dock in its own right at all. The original plan has been described as either being a canal that would provide the adjacent Royal Victoria Dock with an eastern entrance to the river, or nothing more than a plain extension to the Royal Victoria. Whatever the intention, the outcome was a dock of grand proportions, which did indeed provide its older sister, the Royal

Victoria, with a larger entrance. (The original entrance to the west was closed during the 1940s.)

Its engineer was Sir Alexander Rendel, who was best known for constructing railways, having built thousands of miles of line in India and other parts of the Empire. The Royal Albert was highly impressive when it opened for business; it extended to 85 acres, with many millions of bricks used in its construction. Its 3 miles of quay were lined with warehouses.

The Royals, like other docks in London, were protected by walls – or at least by fences and gates. This was largely an attempt to curb pilfering, always endemic in such enterprises. For anybody who had no business to be there, the docks were forbidden territory. Even those in search of work were forced to assemble daily at the dock gates in the hope of attracting the hiring foreman's attention. There was no such thing as job security for labourers.

Now, the entire environment is best described as open-plan. Technically, it must rank as an enormous brownfield site – that is an abandoned, formerly industrial, urban site that has further development potential. If this conjures up depressing images of dereliction and neglect, then a visit to the north quay of the Royal Albert Dock (DLR: Royal Albert) will prove to be an eye-opener.

Although it still awaits the arrival of the developers, the entire site has been levelled, cleared and re-landscaped with paths, grass and trees. It is a very pleasant spot from which to watch arriving and departing aircraft at London City Airport on the opposite side of the dock. It is not unusual to see fish jumping from the water – once an inconceivable thought – an indication of just how much the area has been transformed and cleaned up. The quayside is also a good place from which to appreciate the vast size not just of the Royals, but of Docklands in general. Development around Canary Wharf is certainly impressive, and there is plenty of it; but from the Royals it becomes apparent that Docklands' development potential has barely been touched.

The long-term plan is that this part of the Royals should become a 50-acre business park. There is already outline planning consent for 1.6 million square feet of office space, together with leisure and retail

Building 1000, overlooking the Royal Albert Dock – at the time of writing the only significant new building in the proposed Royals Business Park.

facilities. A limited start has been made, but only in the form of one building – the futuristically named Building 1000, a five-storey structure in glass overlooking the dock. Completed in 2004, it initially was little used, but it was sold in 2007 to the London Borough of Newham, which now uses it as its administrative centre.

The only other noteworthy new development is the Regatta Centre, designed by Ian Ritchie Architects to serve local rowing clubs, and opened in 2000. It is streamlined in appearance, its shape resembling an arrow. The adjoining Albert and Victoria docks form a rowing course that meets international standards.

As with the King George V Dock, only some of the Albert Dock's past remains. This includes the Compressor House, a brick and terracotta building tucked away almost beneath the elevated Royal Albert station. Initially, the Albert dealt in the transhipment of fresh produce and tobacco, together with passenger traffic. However, it was not long before it started to specialise additionally in handling frozen meat; the Compressor House served an adjacent cold store – although this was just a fraction of the enormous capacity of the Royals for chilled and frozen meat.

The former Compressor House, built in 1917. A cold store for more than 300,000 carcasses depended on it.

During the General Strike in 1926, when power cuts were looming, it is estimated that hundreds of thousands of carcasses were at risk throughout the docks. It was the arrival of two Royal Navy submarines that prevented possible disaster. Their generators, whether by design or good fortune, produced precisely the right amount of power to keep the refrigerated stores in service. London, and places further afield, would still get their meat. The motif of the Port of London Authority, picked out in stone, remains proudly displayed above the central entrance to the Compressor House. The building is now used as a business centre but the memory of its former role lives on, as it retains the name 'Compressor House'.

The only other structure remaining from the old days is just beyond the Regatta Centre, at the Connaught Passage, a short channel that connects the Albert and Victoria docks. It is a small building with a pagoda-like roof, bearing some resemblance to a summerhouse – a typical example of the nineteenth-century predilection for using impressive and ornate buildings for even the most utilitarian of functions. This one merely encloses a pumping shaft for the railway tunnel that passes beneath the docks at this point. It served the branch to North Woolwich, which opened in 1847.

Initially a swing-bridge with a span of 90 feet, shared by road and rail traffic, was provided across the passage, but numerous openings for ships meant that delays became more and more frequent. Accordingly, a 600-yard tunnel was opened in 1876, taking the railway line beneath the docks. A steep gradient took it into the tunnel, and so heavy trains that might

The pumping station at the western end of the Royal Albert Dock. It serves the railway tunnel that here passes beneath the Connaught Passage.
The swing-bridge taking the road (but no longer the railway) across the channel is behind it.

stall still used the cross-bridge route. The line across the bridge no longer exists, and the original bridge has been replaced by a more modern one for use solely by road traffic. The North Woolwich line via the tunnel is mothballed, pending construction of the east–west London Crossrail project.

The Royal Victoria Dock

It was in 1850 that the Victoria Dock Company commenced building the Royal Victoria Dock. It opened for business in 1855, boasting a number of innovative features: it was the first dock to be built specifically for steamers (although it still accepted sailing vessels); it was one of the first to have hydraulically operated lock gates, and also one of the first with direct links to the railway network. Its 3 miles of quayside enclosed almost 100 acres of water.

Over the years it became well known for its specialised trades – meat, fruit and tobacco in particular. It had dedicated facilities for each, including a banana berth that at its peak handled millions of bananas weekly. There was also an orange warehouse covering almost 1 acre, while the tobacco warehouses contained up to 20,000 tons of the product.

Although the warehouses were badly bombed during the Second World War, several of the originals remain. There are good, elevated views of these from the raised walkway that leads to the principal entrance to the Excel Exhibition Centre (DLR: Custom House). A string of warehouses lies to the right, variously lettered (in large black characters on a white background) K, N, O, P and R. Comprising two storeys, and built of yellow brick with smart blue window frames and black tiled roofs, they have been finely restored. They date from 1859 and served as bonded tobacco warehouses. Adjacent, warehouse W is taller at four storeys. They all now serve as flats, offices and restaurants.

N, O, P and R warehouses, formerly bonded tobacco warehouses, Royal Victoria Dock.

The Excel Exhibition Centre, standing on the site of the Royal Victoria Dock's custom house. Even though the latter was restored during the 1990s, it was nevertheless demolished to make way for Excel.

Custom House station marks the former site of the custom house, more properly a warehouse, that once stood nearby. With the redevelopment of Docklands, some restoration of the building was undertaken but, despite this, it was in the end demolished, thereby gaining the dubious accolade of being one of the first restored buildings in Docklands, if not the only one, to be pulled down.

Its replacement is by any standards enormous. Completed in 2000, the Excel Exhibition Centre is hard to miss, and its statistics are impressive. The exhibition halls amount to 1 million square feet; the walkway through the centre of the building more resembles a street and is almost 100 feet wide; and, when built, the Centre had, at 285 feet, the United Kingdom's largest single-span roof (a record subsequently lost to Heathrow's Terminal 5). This in turn means that exhibition space is free of pillars. In total, the site amounts to 100 acres and has parking for more than 3,500 vehicles. The Royal Victoria has become an architectural showcase for the bold and the spectacular.

The steps adjacent to the main entrance lead back down to ground (or water) level and Victoria Square, a pleasantly landscaped area

LANDED

One of Docklands' newer artworks is outside the principal entrance to the Excel Centre (DLR: Custom House). *Landed*, by sculptor Les Johnson, was installed in 2009 as a tribute to those who lived and worked in the Royal Docks. Cast in bronze, it shows two dockers, complete with trolley, landing a heavy load under the watchful eye of their foreman.

overlooking the dock. The dockside is lined by cranes, now ornamental rather than functional. The opposite, south quay is lined with more.

However, it is not the cranes that immediately draw the attention here, nor even the exhibition centre, but rather the cantilevered Royal Victoria Dock Bridge across the dock leading to Britannia Village. Opened in 1999 at a cost of almost £4 million, the footbridge is more than 400 feet long and 40 feet high. The two bridge uprights are sunk into the dock floor and contain lifts; for the more energetic, there are eighty steps to the top. It has attracted some criticism for being needlessly high, but for the pedestrian it affords unrivalled views of Docklands, from Canary Wharf in the west, along the length of the Royals to London City Airport in the east. It is hard to imagine that this was once a busy, noisy dock. These days it is an altogether calmer place: apart from the sound of arriving and departing aircraft at London City Airport (under whose flight path the dock is immediately located), the only sound to be heard is the splashing of canoes and kayaks as children enjoy the more sedate activities on offer at the watersports centre at the dock's far western end.

The bridge is often referred to as the 'Transporter Bridge', because the original plan was for a transporter car to be slung beneath the span; that has yet to happen – it would be unique in London. Even that is in danger of being upstaged, as there are now proposals to build a cable car link across the Thames south of the Royal Victoria.

The 'Transporter Bridge' without a transporter, across the Royal Victoria Dock. Britannia Village is in the distance.

BRITANNIA VILLAGE AND SILVERTOWN

THE CABLE-STAYED Royal Victoria Dock Bridge crosses the dock and leads to Britannia Village, a modern development laid out on the principles of a traditional village. It occupies part of what was originally known as West Silvertown. Building commenced, in a small way, in 1994 – although there had been several plans to regenerate the area before then. The property crash of the 1980s meant that none came to fruition.

Eventually, two tower blocks on the south side of the dock were pulled down and replaced initially by a small number of new homes. As confidence returned to the property market, development gradually increased to the effect that almost one thousand new properties – including some in the category of low-cost, 'affordable' housing – were built in the area.

As part of the development deal, the builders were required to contribute towards a village hall and doctors' surgery. Subsequently, a school has also been built, together with a community centre and shops. There is even a green. Hence, Britannia Village is indeed a village in every respect – except that it is in the heart of London's Docklands.

There are ample reminders of this: disused, though carefully preserved cranes – not dissimilar to those on the dock's opposite side – line the quayside. And, this being Docklands, there are naturally a few surprises. Thus, upon leaving the bridge, continue past the

Opposite: D-Silo, Pontoon Dock. The original was destroyed in the Silvertown explosion, this replacement appearing in 1920. Made of concrete, it has a certain degree of elegance about it.

In splendid isolation, this chimney is all that remains of Rank's Empire Mills. The white building in the background is the derelict Spiller's Millennium Mills, awaiting the developer's arrival.

shops, following the signs for Barrier Park; then go through Royal Victoria Place and left into Wesley Avenue. At its eastern end looms a traffic roundabout, in the middle of which, in splendid isolation, is a tall chimney.

The roundabout serves no meaningful purpose at present. It is a precursor of further development to come. The only exit leads into Raleigh Road, then directly into Mill Road, where lies a clue to the chimney's provenance: for this, or more accurately the adjacent Pontoon Dock (an offshoot of the Royal Victoria Dock), was a centre of London's flour-milling industry. Bulk grain arrived at the docks by ship, leaving them as flour, the chimney being all that remains of Rank's Empire Mills. This was one of three flour mills at the dockside, all of which survived in some form until the 1990s, and opened c.1905. It and the Co-operative Wholesale Society's mill have now been demolished; a considerable part of the third, Spiller's Millennium Mills, however, remains. It is one of the few substantial buildings in Docklands left derelict rather than being razed.

Even so, it still presents a formidable sight. There are good views of it from the bridge across Royal Victoria Dock, and from the elevated platforms of nearby Pontoon Dock DLR station. It is also possible to view it more closely by looking out across the hoardings that now surround the site, particularly from Mill Road. The building that remains is large enough, but this was merely the granary.

Its shell, at least, does appear to have a future: suggestions have been made that it should be converted into dwellings. Yet, in a bizarre kind of way, it does not seem entirely out of place as it is,

The north-western part of Britannia Village, as viewed from the Transporter Bridge. The cranes are now the only reminder of how busy the adjacent Victoria Dock used to be.

ruined though it may be. Having been in such a state for so long, it has almost become an accepted part of the landscape.

However, it is not quite all that remains of the milling industry. A few hundred yards beyond the mill is D Silo. It is unmissable, not least because it is rather an odd-shaped structure and is painted white with a large black letter D on it. Dating from 1920, it is made of reinforced concrete and was used for grain storage. Inbound grain was siphoned into it from ships and then discharged on a smaller scale into barges moored in the adjacent Pontoon Dock. The best vantage points are Mill Road and Pontoon Dock station.

The name of Pontoon Dock comes from a period before the area became a centre for milling. Initially, the dock had hydraulic pontoons that raised vessels clear of the water. Emptied of their ballast of water, the pontoons were then able to float to small adjoining docks, with the ship high and dry on top. This function did not, however, survive long; ships simply became too large.

Spiller's Millennium Mills is one of very few remaining derelict buildings in Docklands. The Royal Victoria Dock is to the front, while behind, just visible on the right, is Pontoon Dock. This specialised in handling flour.

Nowadays the adjacent hoardings and the verdancy of North Woolwich Road (to which Mill Road leads) make it hard to see there is a dock here at all. Heading for North Woolwich Road leads to the heart of Silvertown.

Silvertown

Silvertown takes its name from S. W. Silver & Co., a company that established telegraph and rubber works here in 1852. It was no coincidence that they chose this site. The nineteenth century might not be best remembered for environment-protecting legislation, but it nevertheless saw the passing of certain acts that placed stringent restrictions on the establishment of polluting industries within the centre of London.

It so happened that what was to become Silvertown fell just outside the restrictive boundary. Thus, with the benefit of the adjacent river, and the soon-to-arrive docks and rail network, the chemical industry was understandably attracted to the area. The scale of the district's expansion may be gauged from the fact that between 1800 and 1900 the population grew almost fifty-fold to 280,000.

Chemical manufacture flourished; so, too, curiously, did the food-processing industry. Abram Lyle & Sons (of golden syrup fame) arrived in 1883. Their factory is still there, although the present building dates from the 1930s. The nearest station is West Silvertown or, alternatively, walk from Britannia Village, turn right from Mill Road into North Woolwich Road, past the fire station. (There has been a fire station here for almost one hundred years; it was to feature significantly in the area's twentieth-century history – of which more shortly.) More than a million tins of syrup now leave the site each month, and the famous golden syrup tin, first introduced in 1885, has been officially declared the oldest branded product in the world. The company displays what must be the world's largest syrup tin on the factory front. The company's future business partner, Henry Tate & Son, set up shop in 1878 a little further east. With little in the way of environmental health regulations, the combined aromas of both food processing and chemical manufacture must have made Silvertown a very unpleasant place in which to live and work.

Notwithstanding the provision of the Royal Docks, a huge amount of trade was still conducted through the riverside wharves. The old wharf names such as Mohawk, Manhattan, Clyde and Peruvian serve as a reminder that business was truly international. However, it was not trade that made Silvertown famous. Rather, it was what occurred on the premises of Brunner Mond & Co. during January 1917 that propelled the area into the national spotlight. Brunner Mond had arrived in Silvertown in 1894. Here they produced soda crystals. However, with the onset of war in 1914, the plant was all but requisitioned by the government and used for the manufacture of explosives. The site of the factory is variously described as Crescent Wharf (DLR: Pontoon Dock) or Minoco Wharf (DLR: West Silvertown). The two lie adjacent, so it must have been an enormous manufacturing complex.

During the evening of Friday 19 January 1917 fire took hold in Brunner Mond's premises, resulting in the cataclysmic explosion of around 50 tons of TNT. It was the biggest explosion there had then ever been in London; the consequences require little imagination. The fire station in North Woolwich Road was completely destroyed

– it had been built only three years earlier. Several firemen were killed instantly on the premises; more lost their lives fighting the resultant fire at Brunner Mond's plant.

Contemporary reports state that flames were visible from 30 miles away and that the explosion was heard as far away as Southampton – a distance of almost 80 miles. The human cost was inevitably high, although, considering that this was a densely populated area, it is perhaps surprising that only seventy-three lives were lost – both in and around the factory. Almost five hundred were injured. Thousands were made homeless.

The factory, and much of West Silvertown, was levelled. Secondary fires broke out for miles around as the force of the blast ejected burning debris high into the night sky. One of the most spectacular of these was a gasometer in Greenwich, on the opposite side of the river, which erupted in a huge inferno. All told, in excess of sixty thousand premises suffered some kind of damage. Yet, to this day, no

The aftermath of the Silvertown explosion in 1917. This is all that remained of three flour mills, in a picture that appears to have been taken across one of the 'finger docks' that led off Pontoon Dock.

firm explanation has been put forward as to what precisely triggered the events that led to the disaster. Was it, perhaps, wartime sabotage?

Much of the area is derelict or undeveloped today, although Minoco Wharf has been used since Brunner Mond's day, latterly as a refinery and oil-storage site for Shell UK. This ceased during the 1990s, and part of Crescent Wharf now forms the approach to Barrier Park (DLR: Pontoon Dock; see the chapter on 'Parks and Gardens'). Consequently, the site has returned to nature, in a way that only such intensely industrial sites are able; during spring, it is carpeted with wild flowers, awaiting the arrival of the developers – as will surely happen.

The past, however, is not forgotten: a simple obelisk memorial beneath the elevated DLR (adjacent to West Silvertown station) records not just the lives of Brunner Mond employees lost during the disaster, but also those who fell during the First and Second World Wars. For, catastrophic though the Silvertown explosion was, worse was to come later, inflicted by the German air force, and on a much wider scale.

Silvertown had much to attract the Luftwaffe – soft targets and large buildings, among them Tate & Lyle's sugar refinery. As a result, much of the pre-war development here was wiped from the map. Being 180 feet high and the largest cane sugar refinery in the world, the Tate & Lyle works must have made a very tempting target. It was largely rebuilt after the war. The company still refines sugar here, just south of Albert Road, barely 2 miles from the syrup refinery. Access is from the DLR: alight at London City Airport, then take the subway leading to Drew

This must be the largest 907-gram tin of syrup ever. During the Second World War the product was sold in reinforced card cartons owing to the shortage of metal. Lyle's is a long-established company in Silvertown.

Road. The enormous factory lies opposite the end of Saville Road, impossible to miss. Indeed, so huge is the plant that it is easy to forget that just beyond it lies the river, while a little to its north are the docks. This part of Silvertown lies on a relatively narrow strip of dry land between the two.

Tate & Lyle may be a long-established presence in the area, but it is not immune from the march of progress. In June 2010 it was announced that the sugar-refining business (including Lyle's Golden Syrup) had been sold for £211 million to American Sugar Refining. The future of the plants, for the time being at least, is said to be secure.

Much else has changed in Silvertown, too – and continues to do so. The sugar refinery is separated from Albert Road by a disused railway. Closed in 2006, it is all that remains of the former Eastern Counties Railway branch to North Woolwich, which opened in 1847. Silvertown got its own station only in 1863. It was sited a little further west along Albert Road, from where the line veered north-west to pass, via a 600-yard tunnel, beneath the Royal Docks. The course of the line seems likely to be preserved as part of the long-awaited Crossrail scheme linking east and west London. In the interim, the district's rail requirements are served adequately by the Docklands Light Railway.

But, to appreciate the huge changes that this district has undergone, simply turn your back on the refinery and look along the length of Saville Road. As late as the 1950s, the view would, in all likelihood, have been dominated by the sight of an enormous liner towering over the road's small terraced houses. For just beyond the end of the road was a dry dock at the western tip of King George V Dock. It was capable of handling vessels of several tens of thousands of tons.

Nowadays the view is altogether different. Some of the terraced houses remain; a few newer ones have been built. Where the graceful forms of ocean liners and workaday bulk cargo vessels would once have loomed, now lies the apron of London City Airport, with its terminal building. In front of that is an elevated section of the Docklands Light Railway. While much of the King George V Dock remains, the dry dock is no longer visible. As mentioned earlier, the airport's builders merely boxed it in and built over it.

The top end of Saville Road, Silvertown, in 1950. The liner *Dominion Monarch*, 26,263 tons, receives attention in the dry dock of the King George V Dock. Drew Road School is on the right.

Saville Road, in 2010. These buildings would have been behind the photographer in 1950, everything in the photograph above having since been demolished. The walkway to London City Airport and the terminal building beyond provide an echo of the graceful form of the *Dominion Monarch*. The school has been rebuilt one block to the left.

THE ISLE OF DOGS: SOUTH OF CANARY WHARF

THE ISLE OF DOGS is not a natural island, but a peninsula formed as the Thames meanders towards the sea. The closest it has ever come to insular status was with the building in 1805 of the Isle of Dogs Canal, subsequently subsumed into the West India Docks. This effectively severed the island from Poplar to its north, if only by a stretch of dock water. The origin of the Isle's name is uncertain; possibly it is a reference to royal dogs used for hunting in Greenwich Park, on the opposite bank of the river.

While the Canary Wharf development occupies the northern part of the island, the remainder is rather less intensively developed. Like so much of what is now known as Docklands, it is low-lying land. Originally called Stepney Marsh, it was drained by a series of windmills. These stood on an embankment known locally as Mill Wall – a name (albeit as Millwall) still used for much of the district today.

The light railway serves the island well and, after leaving the environs of Canary Wharf and the West India Docks, runs more or less north to south down the middle. Most of the remaining history, heritage and new development lies within a fifteen-minute walk of a DLR station. Thus, from South Quay station, a walk of a few hundred yards west leads to one of the splendid modern footbridges for which Docklands has become renowned.

Opposite: The entrance to South Dock, now the only working lock on the Isle of Dogs. It obligingly opened as this picture, taken from the Blue Bridge, was being composed.

VOWEL OF EARTH DREAMING ITS ROOT/LONDON RIVER MAN
Exit South Quay station and head west along Marsh Wall to find *Vowel of Earth Dreaming Its Root*, an almost chimney-like limestone structure by Eilis O'Connell, near the Manchester Road junction. On the opposite side of Marsh Wall, outside the front windows of an office block, is John W. Mills's *London River Man*, a jolly bronze figure dressed in oilskins and struggling with a heavy-looking load on his shoulders.

The bridge is not easy to find, being hidden by new office development on the north of Marsh Wall midway between Millharbour and Mastmaker Road. However, by walking beneath the here elevated railway and following the footpaths through to South Dock, the explorer will be well rewarded. From a distance, the steel cable-stayed pedestrian bridge over the dock seems almost unremarkable by Docklands' extravagant standards: it is only when

The northern end of Millwall Inner Dock. The connecting channel to the West India Docks was cut only in 1924 and is just out of view, right. Prior to that, the only water link to the river was three-quarters of a mile south-west, via the Outer Dock.

crossing it that it becomes apparent that this is no ordinary bridge. For it wends its away across the water to Canary Wharf in a subtle S-shape.

DOCKLANDS ENTERPRISE
Standing in the water of South Dock, the stainless steel *Docklands Enterprise*, by Wendy Taylor, resembles an intricate knot. Dating from 1987, it is one of the earliest pieces of Docklands art.

By returning east along Marsh Wall and back past South Quay station, good views may be had of Millwall Inner Dock as the road crosses its connection with South Dock – here forming the southernmost part of Canary Wharf. The Inner Dock was the scene of great excitement when parts of the spectacular boat chase in the 1999 James Bond film *The World Is Not Enough* were shot there.

Marsh Wall comes to an end about a quarter of a mile further on at a roundabout forming the junction with Manchester Road. Stewart Street, on the opposite side of the roundabout, leads to a riverside footpath. This is a cul-de-sac but at the end of its brief course south it leads to a big surprise. Admittedly, a storm-water pumping station might hardly be construed as a surprise, but its design is. It has an 'oriental' feel about it; indeed, it looks as if a dragon breathing fire and smoke might emerge from it at any moment. To say that it looks as if it has been built to last is an understatement: there is a huge solidness about it, with its enormous supporting columns. And yet, with fancily painted tracery and colourful brickwork, it conveys an artistic air.

There is no option but to backtrack here and head north towards an unmissable development of flats laid out in the shape of an arc, culminating with taller, stepped blocks at each end. The former of the two is named, somewhat economically, Tower 1; neatly manicured gardens, in an almost minimalistic style, surround them. The entire development is built on the site of a former dry dock. There are good views here both upstream and out across the river to the O2, formerly the Millennium Dome.

In typically extravagant Docklands style, the splendid storm-water pumping station close to Stewart Street.

Much of the development backs on to Manchester Road. Here the dockmaster's offices line the entrance to South Dock where it meets the Thames. The locks forming this entrance still function, thus providing the West India Dock's sole working waterway connection with the river. Manchester Road, meanwhile, crosses the lock by means of a lifting bridge, popularly known as Blue Bridge. Several cranes remain at the lockside as a reminder of the dock's original role.

Shortly beyond South Quay station, the DLR veers south, running parallel with Millwall Inner Dock, best accessed from Mudchute station. Had it not been for the building of the docks, Mudchute – in name, at least – would not exist. Its somewhat insalubrious title is derived from an equally insalubrious activity: liquid mud dredged from the docks was discharged here. Yet Mudchute now forms the Isle of Dogs' green lung; this is covered more comprehensively in the chapter on 'Parks and Gardens'.

Millwall Docks, totalling 36 acres of water, were opened in 1868. They became well known for handling grain, but later were used for wine, timber and fresh produce. Their largest granary had a capacity

Dockmaster's offices at the entrance to South Dock, built in 1929. The neighbourhood would have been less verdant then.

of more than 20,000 tons. Access was via a lock on their western side connecting them to the river. There was never an eastern entrance, and it was not until the early twentieth century that they were connected to their northern neighbours, the West India Docks – thus providing an indirect eastern entrance. These days, there is no direct river access; trade ceased in 1980.

The easiest access to the former docks is by leaving Mudchute station and continuing west along Spindrift Avenue for about 100 yards. Here, an easily missed footpath leads to what was formerly the Millwall Graving Dock, or dry dock. At almost 150 yards long, it was one of London's first, and largest. There is little visible evidence of its former dry-dock role – not least since it is now flooded. Where warehouses and railway tracks once lined the dockside, pleasant houses now stand, part of the Clippers Quay development; where cargo vessels awaited discharge, pontoons, for use by leisure craft, now float.

Beneath these pontoons there is a hidden legacy of the dry dock. The dock sides are formed by a series of steps (the technical term is

The lock gates of the Millwall Docks approaching completion in 1868. Water has yet to be let in. All sign of the lock has now vanished, a slipway having been built in its place.

'altars'), upon which, according to the size of vessel, were rested the wooden stanchions that supported it when the dock was drained, thus preventing it toppling on to its side. The steps lie submerged directly beneath the pontoons; the first 'step' can still be seen by looking down across the railings.

Continuing north for a few hundred yards more leads to the 'junction' of the Millwall Outer Dock, to the west, and Inner Dock. It is marked by a wooden pedestrian bridge – almost medieval in character – crossing the old dry dock. Sadly, it has been out of use for some years. Here, too, is an unusual, if displaced, piece of 'heritage'. It rather resembles an enormous red buoy but it is variously described as part of a pneumatic pump formerly used at the Royal Victoria Dock, or as part of the lifting gear for the locks at the Surrey Docks, on the south side of the river. There is no information panel, and visitors are left to decide for themselves.

Here, too, is a stepped, semicircular 'auditorium' sunk into the grass – a pleasant spot from which to watch proceedings on the adjacent dock waters. The tall chimney just beyond has no industrial legacy, other than that it was once part of a now redundant rubbish incinerator.

A nautical-looking piece of heritage where Millwall Inner and Outer Docks meet. To its right is another isolated Docklands chimney – formerly part of a rubbish incinerator.

The remaining history of this part of the Isle of Dogs (apart from some covered in the chapter on 'Parks and Gardens') is best reached from Island Gardens station. From here, Manchester Road heads west and leads, just a couple of hundred yards later, to the old Millwall fire station. Built in 1904, this is well maintained; a plaque on the wall commemorates two women firefighters who lost their lives during an air raid in 1940. Here, Manchester Road becomes Westferry Road (alternatively accessible from Mudchute station – walk south along Thermopylae Gate, then turn right into Chapel House Street). Here will be found some of the best reminders of one of Docklands' greatest pieces of history.

Isambard Kingdom Brunel's steamship *Great Eastern* was launched in 1858, here at the southern tip of the Isle of Dogs. A monstrous undertaking, it proved to be the death of the great engineer: the entire project was so fraught with difficulty that he suffered a stroke shortly after the vessel's launch. The ship was originally going to be named *Leviathan* – with good reason, being almost 700 feet long, 83 feet wide and with a displacement in excess of 22,000 tons. The vessel was meant to carry four thousand

IN MEMORY OF
JOAN BARTLETT, AGED 18
AND
VIOLET PENGELLY, AGED 19
MEMBERS OF THE AUXILIARY FIRE SERVICE
AMONGST THE FIRST SERVING FIREWOMEN TO DIE ON
DUTY DURING AN AIR RAID
ON
SEPTEMBER 18TH 1940

Above: The old Millwall fire station on Westferry Road, built by the London County Council in 1904. The present fire station is a little further along the road. Left: A commemoration of grimmer times at the old Millwall fire station.

passengers, but this proved to be unattainable since it had to carry so much coal to feed its six boilers that there simply was not room for so many people. It lasted merely five years as a transatlantic liner and then saw service variously as a cable-laying ship and even as an enormous advertising billboard. Its demise came in 1888, when it was broken up, barely thirty years after being launched.

The *Great Eastern* may not have lasted long, but its shipyard and launch site have fared rather better. The ship was laid down at Burrell's Wharf, at John Scott Russell's shipyard – of which, perhaps surprisingly, a considerable amount remains. Scott Russell arrived in Millwall in 1848 when he took over what was then known as the Fairbairn Iron Works. (Over the years, Fairbairn's had gained a reputation as an innovative builder of iron ships.) Scott Russell was responsible for rather more of the *Great Eastern* than is generally credited: as well as supervising the actual construction, he also designed the paddle engines. However, matters did not get off to a good start at Millwall: shortly before construction commenced, the shipyard burned down. It was a portent of things to come.

Shortly after Manchester Road becomes Westferry Road, fingerposts point left to the Thames Path. However, it is worth ignoring these temporarily and continuing for a short distance along Westferry Road. On the left are the three-storey yellow-brick buildings that served as Scott Russell's offices. The company name still appears on them, although they are now occupied by an estate agency. A blue plaque records the site's historical connections, while the adjacent iron gates proclaim that this is Burrell's Wharf – although that name originated after the shipbuilding industry had entered terminal decline. The river is a stone's throw beyond.

Backtracking from here and following the signs to the Thames Path, one soon reaches a small development of modern houses –beyond which are the riverside and Blasker Walk. Blasker Walk and the adjoining Burrell's Wharf were home to a great Docklands curiosity, pink pigeons, although there are none to be seen these days.

The former offices of John Scott Russell, builder of the *Great Eastern*. This building served as the company's counting house.

Burrell & Co. was a firm that manufactured chemical dyes and colours. Already a well-established concern, in 1888 it took over the wharf and workshops that were then here. At first, the site was used for making paint, but the production of dyes became more and more important until, in 1943, paint manufacture ceased entirely. It must have been a slightly unpleasant, if colourful, place to work. Even the smoke and steam from the factory chimneys was red, thus resulting in the pigeons that congregated on the factory roof and chimney assuming a pink hue. Burrell & Co. moved out in 1986; a faded information panel now marks the spot and records the story.

The site where the *Great Eastern* was built is just a few strides further along the riverside. A surprising amount of the old shipyard remains, notably around Burrell's Wharf Square, a series of buildings enclosing what are now pleasant gardens. The centrepiece is the tallest building, Scott Russell's Plate House, an enormous structure

The legacy of Scott Russell remains on Burrell's Wharf, now a pleasant residential area. On the left is the former Plate House; the chimney, now somewhat truncated, served William Fairbairn's ironworks.

With these chains, the *Great Eastern* was finally launched in January 1858. The wooden cross-braces of the launch gear lie in a sunken garden behind the railings in the background.

– at least when compared to those surrounding it. A huge anchor stands in front of it. There is some uncertainty about how the name 'Plate House' came about: it may even date from after Scott Russell's time, when this part of the ironworks was used for the production of plating for ships' hulls.

A tall, octagonal chimney is adjacent to the Plate House: it was built to draw smoke from the ironworks' furnaces. The Plate House has now been tastefully converted to flats, complete with underground car park.

Burrell's Wharf Square is flanked on either side by further flats. The westernmost of these yellow-brick buildings were originally the factory workshops and warehouses of Venesta, makers of wooden boxes. Built considerably later than the Plate House, they stretch from Westferry Road to the waterfront.

The most magnificent legacy of the *Great Eastern*, however, is on the waterfront just beyond the square. Here may be seen enormous wooden beams that formed part of the slipways from which the vessel was eventually launched in 1858, five years after work on it commenced. The ship was launched horizontally, rather than the more traditional stern-first method, mainly because it was feared that the vessel, upon launch, would career straight into the south bank of the river.

The launch proved to be a convoluted affair. The first attempt, on 3 November 1857, was abandoned after several workers were killed or injured by the flailing launch equipment. It took three months and several more failed attempts before success was finally achieved on 31 January the following year.

The remaining cross-braces of the launch equipment are in a slightly sunken garden, fenced off in the interests of safety. Nevertheless, it is still possible to get close up to some of the enormous chains that were used during the launch. The peaceful, raised and developed river embankment of today seems a world away from Brunel's day. Then, this site was little more than a filthy, muddy foreshore of an equally foul river, teeming with activity, and resonating with the incessant din of the riveters' hammers (more than three million rivets were used in the *Great Eastern*).

A few hundred yards further on, the Thames Path is diverted from the riverside and back on to Westferry Road. Continuing along it for about another quarter of a mile as it veers north leads to the old entrance to Millwall Outer Dock. The lock that linked the dock to the river was filled in during 1990, so that there is now no direct access from the dock to the Thames. It has been replaced by an enormously wide concrete slipway, which serves the adjacent Docklands Sailing Centre. The past, however, is not entirely forgotten: part of the operating mechanism of the late-nineteenth-century lock gates is displayed beside the slipway.

Launching the *Great Eastern*. Unfortunately, the original picture caption does not state whether this was the successful launch, or one of the unsuccessful attempts.

BLACKWALL, THE EAST INDIA DOCKS AND POPLAR

THE HONOURABLE EAST INDIA COMPANY was established by royal charter in 1600. It was authorised to trade with south-east Asia (the East Indies) and India – over both of which it held a monopoly. However, it soon came to focus primarily on India. There it became so powerful that, by the eighteenth century, through various means (not least military), it effectively controlled and governed the entire country.

Corruption was rife; individuals made vast fortunes. By the nineteenth century, practically every British person in India was employed by the company – even the soldiers. Additionally, it had its own navy, known as the Bombay Marine. Only in 1858, after the Indian Mutiny, did the country come under the control of the British government – at which time the East India Company ceased trading. Its monopolies had been terminated some years earlier.

Since the beginning, the East India Company's vessels had used the stretch of river around Blackwall (DLR: East India) to discharge their cargoes. Although shipyards and small docks had started to spring up in the area during the seventeenth century, it was the creation of the East India Dock Company, promoted by the East India Company itself, in 1803 that prompted the greatest period of expansion.

Opposite: The principal entrance to the East India Docks, on East India Dock Road. The volume of horse-drawn vehicles would suggest this was before 1913, when the entrance gateway was demolished and the road was widened. A replica was soon built, however.

Almost immediately work started on new docks, under the supervision of John Rennie, the Scottish engineer who also built Waterloo and Southwark bridges and the London Bridge that has since been re-erected in Arizona. The result was separate import and export docks, totalling 27 acres, linked to the Thames by a dock basin.

The East India Company was wealthy, by virtue of the precious commodities (principally tea and spices) in which it traded. It is reputed that in its heyday it handled £30 million worth of tea annually – a colossal amount. Because of the high value of these cargoes, the entire dock system was surrounded by a 20-foot-high wall; yet, unusually, there were no quayside warehouses. Upon arrival, goods were promptly transported to the company's 5 acres of purpose-built warehouses in the City of London.

MERIDIAN METAPHOR

Close to the principal entrance of the old East India Docks, not far from East India station, stands *Meridian Metaphor*. It comprises a series of granite blocks, set out across a plaza overlooking what is left of the old Import Dock. The artwork's title offers a clue to its precise location: the prime meridian, zero degrees longitude, passes through the site. The sculpture seems popular with office workers, who use the blocks as lunchtime seats – although that may not have been the intention of the artist, David Jacobson.

Almost adjacent, practically at the water's edge, is *Renaissance,* a large bronze figure, by Maurice Blik, of a man and a woman seemingly dancing in a surreal kind of way.

The East India Docks

Although most of the old dock area has been redeveloped, there are many reminders of its past. These are best accessed by crossing Aspen Way, an extremely busy road, by the footbridge leading from East India station. Immediately at its end, to the left, is a fine section of the original Import Dock walls. On the Naval Row side (that is, not

Fine stretches of the old dock walls remain at the East India Docks. This section is at the eastern end of Naval Row. The building behind is typical of the development that has now all but obliterated the docks.

within the former confines of the walls), several nineteenth-century buildings remain; the most impressive of these is the hydraulic pumping station, enclosed by iron railings and with an elegant tower at its eastern end. It has been tastefully converted into homes.

Walking north beyond the walls into the old dock area leads to what is left of the Import Dock. This, with attendant greenery and fountain, now serves as an ornamental lake – a little green lung amid the extensive redevelopment. The Export Dock, only about half the size of the Import Dock, barely survived the Second World War, being infilled with bombing debris shortly afterwards. A power station replaced it, but even that has since been demolished and replaced by residential development.

The Import Dock also underwent changes during the war; part of it was drained and used for constructing Mulberry harbours, the temporary structures that were floated across the English Channel as part of the D-Day operation. However, it was not until the East India Docks finally closed for business in 1967 that this part was

All that remains of the East India Import Dock. It is hard to imagine that this was once a thriving place of trade for one of the most powerful companies in the world.

filled in. Modern office blocks now stand on the site, including the building (with more than a hint of Art Deco about it) that serves as the town hall for the London Borough of Tower Hamlets.

The dock's past, however, is reflected in the new development's street names: Saffron Avenue, Coriander Avenue and Clove Crescent (around which most of the smart new offices have been built), to name but a few. Even a little water remains in the heart of the new development – strictly ornamental, man-made and of the post-dock era – in the form of a narrow stream along the southern side of Clove Crescent.

SHADOW PLAY
At Compass House, on the corner of Clove Crescent, Dave King's *Shadow Play* – apparently cut from steel sheet – depicts dockers in silhouette going about their business.

Further stretches of the old dock walls survive at the opposite end of the site on the western side of Leamouth Road. (Walk east along Saffron Avenue, turn left into Oregano Drive, then right into Sorrel Lane.) In total, the East India Docks probably have more dock walls remaining than the rest of Docklands put together. Impressive though they are, even these pale into insignificance compared to what lies on the other side of Leamouth Road. At first glance, it almost resembles a grand entrance to some sort of temple; then again, with its raised wooden gate, it could pass as the entrance to a particularly well-fortified castle. It is a solidly built structure with a stone tower on each side of the gateway giving the impression that its role was to keep people out: and that, indeed, was the case. For this is the rebuilt entrance to the East India Company's pepper warehouses – a rarity on two counts. Firstly, it is one of the few original buildings to survive here (or at least, part of one); and secondly, most of the company's warehouses were situated in the City. Surprisingly, perhaps, it was deemed that pepper was not

The entrance to the old pepper warehouse, Leamouth Road. There are further fine stretches of dock wall immediately behind the photographer.

sufficiently valuable to be hastily transported there; looking at the robustness of the gate, one might wonder whether the company had second thoughts about this theory.

Nothing remains of the warehouses: they fell prey to wartime bombs, and the gateway itself has been rebuilt as part of the area's redevelopment a short distance from its original site. Nevertheless, it remains a sterling reminder of the district's heritage – even if it does not lead anywhere.

Leaving the area of the old Import Dock by means of the pedestrian bridge across Aspen Way leads back to East India station. Blackwall Road, a much quieter street, follows the course of the elevated railway north-east. However, matters concerning the West merit a brief detour. The street names provide a clue: Jamestown Way, Newport Avenue, Pilgrims Mews.

Thus, leave the vicinity of the station by crossing Blackwall Way, then go straight into Newport Avenue. Much of the development here stands on the site of a former power station (1956–88), which in turn stood on the site of the East India Company's Export Dock. Walk past the children's play area and make a right turn into Jamestown Way – or, more simply, just head for the river. There is

ELECTRON
A short walk east along Blackwall Way from East India station leads to a large block of residential apartments. They are overlooked by the elevated railway and a piece of artwork, *Electron*, erected in 2002, which rather resembles a huge bolt of lightning.

a broad embankment here, lined by new apartments, one of several changes that the area has seen over the years.

However, the most momentous event to have taken place in these parts is recorded by a grand riverside monument. It was from hereabouts, on 19 December 1606, that 105 'adventurers' aboard the *Susan Constant*, *Godspeed* and *Discovery* sailed for the New World. More than four months later, they landed at Cape Henry in Virginia, and two weeks after that they reached Jamestown. The expedition was led, aboard the *Susan Constant*, by Captain Christopher Newport. This was the first of five voyages he made to Virginia, the last being in 1611. He was appointed vice-admiral of the colony in 1610.

The monument is a replacement for the original, which was erected nearby in 1928. That had a mermaid on top of the plinth, but it was vandalised and stolen many years ago. The current version is topped with an astrolabe – an early navigational instrument.

The Thames-side monument to seventeenth-century American settlers. The builders of the adjacent new development have named it, appropriately, Virginia Quay.

Looking upstream from here, it is just possible to see the lock gates leading to an old dry dock. Back on Blackwall Way, however, it is hard to miss the signs pointing east to Trinity Buoy Wharf. There are so many of them that the impression is given that this is something that should not be missed, and, although it is out of the way, Trinity Buoy Wharf is well worth the ten-minute walk from East India station.

Trinity Buoy Wharf

The signs lead to a busy roundabout, adjacent to which is the only wholly surviving part of the former East India Docks system – the East India Dock Basin. This is covered comprehensively in the chapter on 'Parks and Gardens'. Briefly follow the dual carriageway, keeping the dock basin to the right, then fork right along Orchard Place (thus named because there once was an orchard here), still following the signs for Trinity Buoy Wharf. A large black, red and white buoy, upon which is emblazoned 'Trinity Wharf', announces that you have arrived.

It would be far from accurate to say that Trinity Buoy Wharf is preserved in a time warp – but it is the closest that anywhere in Docklands comes to that, for here will be found the greatest concentration of original Docklands buildings in any one place. There are, nevertheless, parts of the wharf that are as modern and surprising as anywhere else. It lies on a small peninsula formed where the River Lea (here known as Bow Creek) joins the Thames. As its name implies, the locality has a history strongly associated with the Corporation of Trinity House, the organisation responsible for lighthouses and lightships.

The first records of Trinity House being on this site date back to the mid-eighteenth century, although only from 1803 did it have a continuous presence here. By then, workshops for the manufacture of buoys had begun to appear. Activity increased apace: further buildings were added until, at its peak, the wharf was responsible not only for buoys, but also for servicing lightships based throughout south-east England. (However, this was not the corporation's head office: that was at Tower Hill, almost opposite the Tower of London.)

Such activity lasted until 1988, when Trinity House pulled out of the area. Initially taken over by the London Docklands Development Corporation, the site was eventually leased, in 1998, to Urban Space Management, a company that specialises in urban regeneration. (Other projects include the Camden Lock development.) The result of that company's work has been the establishment of what is best described as an arts and cultural quarter, with studios, offices, 'live and work space', and places for performances and exhibitions. But it is an arts quarter with a difference, for not only have many of the old buildings been put to good use (and due deference paid to their heritage), but one or two newcomers have also arrived. As a result, the locality has proved extremely popular with film-makers.

A tour is best undertaken in a circular fashion. The approach along Orchard Place is lined, on the right, by workshops dating from the 1950s. Arrival at Trinity Buoy Wharf proper is signalled by an enormous anchor, immediately in front of what now serves as a visitor centre (usually open weekends only). This particular building was originally the wharf's gatehouse.

Almost immediately ahead is one of the newer arrivals – Fatboy's Diner, a structure adorned in chrome, with more than a hint of the United States about it. This is hardly surprising, as it was built in New Jersey in 1942. It featured in the 1998 film *Sliding Doors*, when Gwyneth Paltrow was a customer. The diner is on the wharf fronting the River Lea, and it is hereabouts that much of the Trinity House heritage has been commendably maintained – not least with the arrival of a former lightship that was built in 1938.

The experimental lighthouse at Trinity Buoy Wharf. This is the second lighthouse to stand on the site; the chain and buoy store is immediately behind it.

London's only lighthouse is adjacent to the confluence of the Thames and the Lea. Dating from 1864, it was not built as an aid to navigation *per se*, but used for testing purposes. (It was not the first light to be erected here: an earlier one was built in 1854, although that had been removed by 1930.) In those days the use of electricity as a means of illumination was in its infancy, and Michael Faraday, a scientific advisor to Trinity House, conducted experiments in the earlier lighthouse. As a result of these, electrical lighting was subsequently installed in 1858 at South Foreland lighthouse in Kent – Britain's first to be electrically lit.

The lighthouse is attached to the chain and buoy store, also dating from 1864 – its purpose as implied. These days it is used as an entertainment and exhibition venue; it had one spectacular moment of fame as a restaurant when Pierce Brosnan made a typically James Bond exit in the film *The World Is Not Enough*.

Other buildings include the electricians' shop (the oldest building on the site, 1835) and the boilermakers' house. The most unusual structures, however – and what could be more unusual than a lighthouse in London – are hard to miss. They are bright, colourful and resemble shipping containers that have been stacked on top of each other. While the use of shipping containers as dwelling space is a concept more conventionally associated with the developing world, that is precisely what they are.

There are three separate 'Container City' buildings. Those in Cities I and II have walls a mere 2 mm thick, their robustness coming from their corrugation and their reinforced corners. They still weigh 4 tonnes each, however. Container City III, or the Riverside Building, at 15,000 square feet, is the most recently built (2005) and looks out across the Thames. Still obviously container-like in appearance, the fronts have been replaced principally by glass – thus affording panoramic views across the river to the O2, which seems almost within touching distance. Circular, porthole-type windows maintain the nautical theme in Container Cities I and II.

This is not the only form of recycling on the site; the pontoon of its pier (Jubilee Pier) formerly saw service as a Thames lighter, while

Container City 'live and work' space gives a new meaning to the term 'self-contained'.

its walkway was once part of a North Sea oil-rig. Even the information panels are made from shipping container doors.

Hidden behind the riverside containers is one further legacy of the past – the proving house, built in 1870. This single-storey building has a hint of rural stables about it. It is extremely long, too, and with good reason – for it was here that the strength of chains used on buoys was tested.

Trinity Buoy Wharf, however, is just one part of the story of Bow Creek. Shipbuilding, on both sides of the river, has also played a significant role in the area's history, although few legacies of this remain. The best-known of the shipbuilders was the Thames Ironworks, or, more properly, the Thames Iron Works & Shipbuilding & Engineering Company Ltd. It arrived here in 1857, but the ironworks had been founded much earlier as Ditchburn & Mare, whose original yard was along Orchard Place.

Business prospered, resulting in the company, now known as C. J. Mare & Co., expanding on to the opposite side of Bow Creek towards Canning Town. Then, for a variety of reasons, the company ran into difficulties until, in 1857, the Thames Ironworks took over.

At its peak, the company occupied 30 acres; a chain ferry across the River Lea connected both sites. Initially, it specialised in building smaller, lighter vessels – including 250 lifeboats (many of which were destined for the RNLI). However, with expansion on to the more capacious eastern side of Bow Creek, the Thames Ironworks was able to undertake larger enterprises, so that it eventually added warships and almost three hundred merchant vessels to its tally.

The climax of the yard's history, however, came in May 1859 when the Admiralty commissioned the building of HMS *Warrior*, the Royal Navy's first ironclad steam frigate. Launched in 1860, it was one of the largest vessels of the day, with a displacement of almost 9,200 tons. Its armour was more than 4 inches thick. A large piece of this has been incorporated into a memorial to the shipyard on the wall of the stairs leading to Canning Town station (DLR and London Underground Jubilee Line). *Warrior* is preserved at Portsmouth as a museum ship.

At one time more than three thousand workers were employed in the yard. After initial difficulties with labour relations, it became

This memorial and a piece of platework from HMS *Warrior* on the steps leading to Canning Town station commemorate the Thames Ironworks and the district's shipbuilding heritage.

renowned for treating its workers well, especially by establishing sports clubs. Thus was formed, in 1895, the Thames Ironworks Football Club. Its players, it transpired, were rather good; by the end of the century, they had turned professional – having long been known by their nickname of the Hammers. Today, the club is known as West Ham United, whose crest, bearing ironworkers' hammers, is a reminder of its roots.

The end of the Thames Ironworks came suddenly. With an ever-increasing requirement for larger and larger vessels, the yard simply was not big enough. Launching was becoming increasingly awkward – a reality that was tragically driven home in 1898 when HMS *Albion* was launched. The enormous wave and wash created drowned thirty-seven spectators.

In 1910 the Royal Navy commissioned HMS *Thunderer*, another behemoth of a vessel at 22,500 tons. Although successfully launched the following year, it was to be the straw that broke the camel's back. Struggling to compete with larger shipyards elsewhere in Britain, the Thames Ironworks became insolvent shortly afterwards, and ceased trading.

Poplar

Poplar Dock (DLR: Blackwall) lies at the eastern extremity of the West India Docks. It has seen a variety of uses, including, initially, as a reservoir to regulate the water level in the nearby West India Docks, and as a timber pond – storing timber afloat prevented it from warping.

During the 1840s, in response to the fuel-hungry industries that had developed throughout the East End, limited docking facilities were added, thus enabling coal to be imported from north-east England. By 1851 the former timber ponds and reservoirs had become proper, fully functioning docks. As well as this, they had also become London's first docks to be served by rail, in a joint venture by the East and West India Dock companies and the Birmingham Junction Railway Company. It became the North London Railway in 1853. Being rail-served drew additional trade and, although the

Poplar Dock, now home to a pleasant marina. The travelling cranes would have been rail-mounted.

majority of London's principal docks were eventually connected to the rail network, Poplar remained unique in that its rail system was the only one not to be absorbed by the Port of London Authority.

Poplar Dock and the surrounding area suffered huge damage during the Second World War. However, on cessation of hostilities, trade continued – principally in coal and steel. However, it was always one of London's smaller docks and inevitably, with the passage of time, trade suffered. By 1981 Poplar Dock had closed for business, much of it being filled in. However, what was left underwent yet another change of use when, in 1999, a new ninety-berth leisure marina was opened.

> **FIGUREHEADS FOR DOCKLANDS**
> On the north-eastern corner of Poplar Dock, *Figurehead for Docklands* by Anna Bisset is an exuberant-looking figure made of what is best described as punctured sheets of metal. There are probably rather more holes than metal, but it is an extremely eye-catching work.

However, sufficient of its past remains to serve as a reminder of its former role. The dock is best accessed by exiting Blackwall station and using the spiralled subway beneath Aspen Way. On the west side of the dock, two of the original red travelling cranes remain – now almost dwarfed by modern waterside apartments. A fine stretch of the dock wall also remains on the east side of what is now the marina.

Walking along this side of the dock eventually leads back on to Preston's Road; following this for a couple of hundred yards south

The now leafy Bridge House was once home to the Head Dockmaster of the West India Dock Company. The Blackwall Basin lies to its left, Poplar Dock behind.

leads to the entrance lock to Blackwall Basin, which, in turn, connects with both Poplar Dock and West India Dock. The lock is now non-functional, but the nineteenth-century Bridge House, hidden behind a canopy of foliage on the lock's northern side, remains. This served as the home of the superintendent of the West India Dock Company.

Just beyond, a little further south and on the right, is all that remains of the old Blackwall Basin graving, or dry, dock. Filled with water, it is now purely ornamental and is crossed by Lovegrove Walk. Like so many other places in Docklands, it is also home to works of public art.

LEAP

Near the entrance basin of the Blackwall graving dock is one of Docklands' earliest pieces of art, *Leap* – a series of dolphins sitting in the water, the work of Franta Belsky. It dates from the early 1980s.

CANARY WHARF
AND RIVERSIDE

THIS IS WHERE a large-scale map is extremely handy. Without one, attempting to navigate this relatively small area is almost impossible; even then, there is an element of hit and miss.

Firstly, the name 'Canary Wharf' needs clarification. For many it conjures up images of the tower that is more correctly known as Number One, Canada Square. That is indeed part of what is now referred to as the Canary Wharf Estate, an area of almost 100 acres at the northern end of the Isle of Dogs that is administered by the Canary Wharf Group PLC.

The original wharf that bore the name 'Canary Wharf' formed part of the West India Import Dock. Within the context of the West India Docks' history, it is a name that is relatively new: it did not appear until 1937, when a warehouse was built to replace two that had burned down some years earlier, with the reputed loss of thousands of gallons of rum. This new warehouse, however, was to be used for imported fruit from the Canary Islands; thus the adjacent wharf acquired its name – a name picked out in large letters on one of its warehouses.

The wharf, however, was just a very small part of the West India Docks system – arguably the jewel in the crown of London's old docks. There were three principal docks: the Import, Export and

Opposite: Admire the architecture from a distance. The view from Preston's Road, about half a mile from the centre of Canary Wharf, looking across Blackwall Basin. The giants are all here: the tower, the Citi building, the Barclays building and, just showing behind it, the HSBC building.

South docks, set in that order from north to south at the northern
end of the Isle of Dogs. They were built specifically to handle cargo
from the West Indies.

As early as 1793, a group of London merchants, under the
leadership of a planter named Robert Milligan, recognised the need
for a secure, walled system of docks to handle these cargoes, which
were often of high value. Thus, the Import Dock was open by 1802;
the Export Dock followed four years later. South Dock started
functioning as a dock in 1829, although it had originally opened at
the beginning of the century as a canal – the Isle of Dogs Canal. It
sliced straight through the Isle of Dogs from east to west, thus saving
a time-consuming detour around the peninsula for vessels bound
further upstream.

The docks ceased trading in 1980, shortly after which the London
Docklands Development Corporation made them the principal focus
of regeneration in the area. Initially progress was slow, but building

Inspiration for things to come: Canary Wharf as it was in 1952.

gained a greater momentum with the completion of the Docklands Light Railway in the area in 1987; the first tenants moved in during 1991. Now, despite recessions, bankruptcies and much uncertainty, Canary Wharf thrives. Almost 100,000 people (many in the financial services industry) work here in a variety of sometimes grand office buildings. They are served by an outstanding public transport network, several shopping malls and almost two hundred shops.

The best way to investigate Canary Wharf is to alight at West India Quay station. It is far easier to establish bearings from here, and it is also handily placed for finding some of the district's remaining older buildings. However, before leaving the station, it is worth looking east from its elevated position for good views of Billingsgate fish market. This moved here from its former site adjacent to London Bridge in 1982 and is one of Docklands' earliest examples of regeneration.

Exiting the station and walking west immediately leads to West India Quay and the former West India Import Dock. Several of the original cranes have been preserved here, and although

they are impressively tall they are dwarfed by the adjacent building, the London Marriott Hotel. Designed by HOK architects, it is clad in dark glass, and is thirty-three storeys high and almost scimitar-shaped, as is its ground-floor restaurant, named Curve. The lower storeys serve as the hotel; the remainder are residential apartments.

The rest of the Import Dock is lined on its northern side by old yellow-brick warehouses. The taller ones extend to five floors and most,

Warehouses, West India Docks. A small section of the old dock walls remains just to the right of the footway.

with the exception of Number 1 Warehouse, have been converted to retail and restaurant use. During the summer months, this is a hugely popular place for alfresco eating – so much so that it can be difficult to appreciate the architecture's true form behind the parasols, tables and chairs. For a better, if somewhat less colourful view, it is best to walk along Hertsmere Road to the rear of the warehouses.

Number 1 Warehouse, meanwhile, is the perfect home for the outstanding Museum of London Docklands, a subsidiary of the Museum of London. However, it is not solely a museum *of* Docklands; it is far more than that, and comprehensively tells the story of London as a port from before Roman times to the present day. Topics covered include the sugar trade (Number 1 Warehouse was formerly a sugar warehouse) and Docklands at war; 'Sailortown' is an excellent walk-through re-creation of nineteenth-century Wapping.

MUSEUM OF LONDON DOCKLANDS INFORMATION:
Museum of London Docklands, West India Quay, London E14 4AL.
Telephone: 020 7001 9844. Website: www.museumindocklands.org.uk
Open daily (except 24–26 December), 10 a.m. to 6 p.m.
Admission free.

Along the quayside a small selection of marker buoys maintain the nautical theme, while on the water itself several historic boats have found a home. These include the tugs *Knocker White*, built in 1924, and *Varlet*, built in 1935. However, the most unusual vessel is a barge, *St Peter's Barge*, London's only floating church.

Midway along the Import Dock, a pale green pedestrian footbridge leads to Canary Wharf proper (West India Quay does not form part of the Canary Wharf Estate). This is a floating bridge, moored to pontoons. These are invariably covered in coins – an example of that curious tradition of tossing coins into the water for good luck.

At the far western end of the Import Dock, a bronze statue of Robert Milligan surveys proceedings, while adjacent is a small-scale replica of the dock's original entrance. Exiting the quayside here leads immediately to Hertsmere Road, on the opposite side of which is a curious, extremely small, circular domed building. In recent years it has seen service as a newsagent's shop, but its original role was as a guardhouse. One of two that were originally built in 1805, it was used by the dock's military guard.

Turning right into Hertsmere Road leads to a small preserved section of the dock wall. This is graced by an enormous stone tablet proclaiming the wondrousness of the enterprise and its founders. Not content with a wall, they also built a moat

The so-called Dockmaster's House was never anything of the sort. It is now used as a restaurant.

around the dock's perimeter, although nothing remains of this now. Opposite the wall, on the corner of Garford Street and overlooked by the elevated DLR, is Dockmaster's House. It is Georgian in style and, although it bears the crest of the Port of London Authority (dated 1928), it was built in 1807. Despite its name, it was used as an excise office, then as a tavern; it is now a restaurant. Almost on its doorstep are two of the dock's three original gate piers.

Around 20 yards north of Dockmaster's House, the DLR passes overhead. Briefly following its path leads to Garford Street, a narrow road heading west. On the left-hand side is a row of small dark-brick cottages. These date from the early nineteenth century and originally served as homes for members of the dock's private police force. The centre cottage, the largest of the three, was for the sergeant.

By the late eighteenth century it was estimated that more than £500,000 worth of goods was being stolen from London's docks each year. With the building of the enclosed docks, the problem

Dock constables' cottages in Garford Street.

eased considerably, but even so the losses suffered – particularly by the West India Company – were considered sufficiently high to merit the establishment, at considerable cost, of its own police force. This was to be a course of action that most other dock companies followed almost immediately, each docking concern thus becoming responsible for its own police force. The forces were all merged under the stewardship of the Port of London Authority in 1909.

Garford Street leads to Westferry Road, and a busy junction serving the Limehouse Link – a tunnel that passes under Limehouse Basin, and one of the principal routes from Docklands to the City. Crossing Westferry Road by means of the pedestrian-controlled traffic lights leads to a pathway to the left of the Limehouse Link, and this in turn leads to the Thames Path. A right turn here along the path leads to a mix of old and new architecture. The riverside has been redeveloped almost in its entirety, as represented by a range of apartments highlighted by an eleven-storey girdered tower whose balconies and walkways stand almost detached from the main building. They look across the river like a rocket poised for launch.

Do not be surprised if you hear voices here – even if there is not a soul in sight. They merely come from *Speaking of the River*, a stainless steel audio seat that continuously relates riverside tales of times past – albeit in a slightly eerie manner.

Beyond that, the Thames Path is carried west on another of Docklands' typically extravagant masted footbridges as it crosses Limekiln Dock. The dock is tidal, and typical of many similar that were once common on the Thames.

Left: These riverside flats, adjacent to the Thames Path, date from 1997. The stainless steel seat, bottom right, is similar to *Speaking of the River*, the audio seat situated a little earlier along the path.

Below: The single-masted stayed footbridge, part of the Thames Path, across Limekiln Dock, which is to the right. This is a popular route for lunchtime joggers.

Dunbar Wharf, whose old, restored warehouses line the dock, is named after Duncan Dunbar, a nineteenth-century shipping company whose vessels sailed the world from here.

Walking back towards Canary Wharf, there are good views downstream, not least of Cascades Tower, one of the very first residential developments to be built (1988), which in profile rather resembles an isosceles triangle, and whose various floors do indeed appear to 'cascade'. It stands on the south side of the former South Dock lock entrance.

Broad sweeps of steps lead from the riverside towards Westferry Circus, from where it is a short walk to the *Traffic Light Tree* at Heron Quay. A road traffic security control point guards the entrance to Heron Quay, where scenes from the film *Basic Instinct II* were shot. Here, too, will be found one of Docklands' most unusual commemorative plaques. Located at the entrance to Heron Quays station ('Quays' for the station but, strangely, merely 'Quay' for the street), it tells its own story: 'This plaque marks the spot where on Sunday 27 June 1982 Captain Harry Gee of Brymon Airways landed his DHC Dash 7 on Heron Quay.'

The *Traffic Light Tree*, by Pierre Vivant, on the roundabout linking Westferry Road with Heron Quay, as the name suggests, is an enormous 'tree' (although not a real one), on whose 'branches' are mounted numerous sets of working traffic lights. They change colour at random and serve no purpose other than to entertain the bystander – and perhaps to confuse any unwary motorist who might encounter them.

Therefore, the first aircraft landing in Docklands was not at London City Airport. That had then barely entered the planning stages, but it nevertheless proved that an airport in Docklands was not as far-fetched as some might have imagined. It also demonstrates graphically how this district has changed: these days there would not even be room to park an aircraft, let alone land one. Brymon, meanwhile, became one of the first airlines to operate from City Airport.

The Canary Wharf Estate

Canary Wharf has justifiably gained a reputation for its spectacular architecture. The mighty tower – Number One, Canada Square – is the centre of attention, but the adjacent Citi, HSBC and Barclays towers are just as impressive. The Citi tower, forty-two storeys high and with 1 million square feet of office space, is home to the United States bank Citigroup. The tower was sold in 2007 for £1 billion. The similarly sized HSBC tower changed hands in 2009 for almost £750 million.

But it is One, Canada Square that is the signature image of the development. The work of American architect Cesar Pelli, and originally named the Canary Wharf Tower, it was the first building of any size to be completed here – its first occupants arriving in 1992. At that time, it was Britain's tallest building, soaring more than 800 feet skywards. Its other statistics are, not surprisingly, impressive – not least in that it has fifty floors and almost four thousand

The tower: One, Canada Square as seen across the water from South Dock. The buildings overlooking the water are on the south-west corner of Cabot Square, which, like the tower, was one of the first parts of Canary Wharf to be developed.

windows. The entire building will purportedly (and intentionally) sway 13 inches – if the winds are strong enough.

The ground floor, meanwhile, is the only part of the building that is accessible to the public – effectively forming a short cut from North Colonnade to South Colonnade. However, it is all too easy to be entirely unaware that it is the 'Tower' through which you have walked. (The author walked, or thinks he walked, through on several occasions before realising.) And thereby lies the catch with Canary Wharf: everything is huge. And everything is relatively tightly packed; finding a particular building – especially the very tall ones – is difficult. At ground level, it is hard to pick out defining features; they appear much higher up. So, while it is undoubtedly an awe-inspiring experience to stand at the base of One, Canada Square and stare 800 feet skywards, the greater intricacies of the architecture and, indeed, the sheer majesty of the place, are better viewed from a distance. The DLR stations at Westferry and Poplar are good spots, as is looking along Blackwall Basin from Preston's Road. The view across South Dock from Marsh Wall is also good.

That is not to say that the centre of Canary Wharf should be avoided. On the contrary, it is an experience not to be missed – especially on weekdays when the atmosphere created by a cocktail of fine architecture and thousands of people bustling about their business is unlike anywhere else in London.

With almost a blank canvas to work on, and little in the way of conservation issues to distract them, the estate has drawn the world's greatest architects. As well as Cesar Pelli (who is responsible for several other buildings here), there are buildings by Terry Farrell and Partners, Foster and Partners (for example, 15 Westferry Circus and Nos 8 and 33 Canada Square), and several others besides. What makes their work all the more remarkable is that the majority of the estate is built over, or in, old docks. Hence, the area of water remaining today is considerably less than when the docks were built.

The various shopping malls are a prime example of this – most being beneath ground. Or so it would seem: they have simply been built within the old docks. All the usual names are here, as well as many up-market brands – befitting Canary Wharf's status as one of

Not all the great architecture at Canary Wharf reaches for the sky. Banks of escalators, bathed in natural light, head for ground level at Canary Wharf Underground station.

the world's leading financial districts. In matters of shopping, the moral here would appear to be the same as elsewhere at Canary Wharf: notwithstanding a preponderance of maps about the estate, be prepared to get lost, especially beneath ground, in a pleasurable kind of way. Allow a certain amount of time to visit, and consider it a job well done if you get away within twice that amount.

The building in or over docks continues at the eastern end of West India Import Dock, where work has commenced on the new Crossrail station. However, the finest example of in-dock architecture opened in 1999 as part of London Underground's Jubilee Line extension.

Canary Wharf Underground station, designed by Foster and Partners, is built within a drained dock: more specifically, it is contained within a 325-yard-long concrete box that has been sunk into the dock and then 'pegged' in place with huge piles. If laid flat, One, Canada Square would fit inside with room to spare. The station's cavernous form is a masterpiece of steel and glass, the ticket hall alone being 243 yards long. From ground level, it is unobtrusive, minimalistic almost – its two principal, glass-roofed entrances projecting rather like raised eyebrows. These cleverly allow natural light to flood into the station – where a scene from the 2003 film *Love Actually* was shot. Eight enormous escalators link the ticket hall with ground level, 90 feet above. Riding these as they gracefully descend into the cathedral-like concourse is one of the defining experiences of discovering London's Docklands.

PARKS AND GARDENS

I F THE ARCHITECTURE throughout Docklands is noteworthy in scope and style, so too are its open spaces. They range from the long-established (those that arrived at the same time as heavy industry), through the converted (abandoned industrial features that now serve as recreational sites), to the purpose-built, neatly formalised and manicured gardens of the twentieth century.

Mudchute Park

Mudchute and Millwall Parks effectively merge into one, the former being the more northerly, situated on the eastern side of East Ferry Road, opposite Mudchute station.

The broad footpath known as Globe Rope Walk, running west to east, is the closest there is to a boundary between them and takes its name from the former Globe rope works, opened here in 1881 by Hawkins & Tipson. In the days of sail, and to a lesser degree, later, there was a huge demand for rope. Short lengths being of little use to anybody, the manufacturing process required a long site, known as a rope walk. In this particular factory, the rope was made using a rail-mounted piece of machinery, known as a traveller, that ran the ropewalk's length of almost a quarter of a mile – that is, practically the entire width of what is now Mudchute Park. Hawkins & Tipson specialised in manufacturing rope for the maritime trade, mainly

Opposite: Clean-cut angles at Barrier Park. The Barrier Point development forms a complementary backdrop.

using sisal, hemp and manila. It was only in 1957 that the company experimented with synthetic fibres; these were principally made at a long-established plant at Hailsham, in East Sussex, where the company had also been trading since 1941. It sold the resultant product under the brand name of 'Marlow', and the company soon came to be known as Marlow Ropes.

The Hawkins & Tipson plant at Mudchute survived until 1971, when all operations were transferred to East Sussex. All trace of the factory has been obliterated. Marlow Ropes, meanwhile, has been sold and split up, but the manufacture of ropes still continues under the Marlow brand, a worthy descendant of Hawkins & Tipson.

A few hundred yards north of the eastern end of Globe Rope Walk is Mudchute City Farm – the largest city farm in London (open Tuesday to Sunday, admission free). Established in 1977 and

Millwall Park. Globe Rope Walk and the site of the Globe rope works follow the entire length of the tree line in the middle distance as the path sweeps right. Mudchute Park lies beyond.

Mudchute Farm. The Canary Wharf office blocks are less than a mile away.

extending over 32 acres, it is home to around two hundred animals. Around the farm, the terrain rises sharply in irregular-sized mounds – the result of siphoning operations during the dredging of the nearby Millwall Docks.

As elsewhere in Docklands, the district suffered badly during the Second World War. Further battles followed, not least against proposals to build tower blocks in the area. Popular pressure thwarted these plans, leaving Mudchute to develop into the pleasant green area it is today.

Millwall Park

Millwall Park is immediately to the south of Globe Rope Walk, comprising largely playing fields, with some wild-flower areas. Between 1901 and 1910 the north-western quadrant of the park was the home of Millwall Football Club, the Isle of Dogs' professional team. (Originally, it is thought to have been the team of a processed food factory.) The underlying dredged mud can hardly have made it an ideal site.

Running north-west to south-east through the edge of the park is an arched railway viaduct that, in the normal course of events, would hardly merit a second glance. It is best viewed at a distance, from Globe Rope Walk. However, there is something a little unusual about it: it leads nowhere, being truncated at each end.

It was not always thus – even if it has spent more of its existence disused than in service. Originally 682 yards long, the single track Millwall Park Viaduct formed part of the Millwall Extension Railway. This ran broadly north to south through the Isle of Dogs, connecting Poplar on the London & Blackwall Railway with North Greenwich (from where ferries crossed to the river's south bank). Although the line was authorised by act of Parliament in 1865, it was not until 1871 that it was opened throughout – principally because of rivals' objections. Even so, it was a remarkably long time for a line little more than 1½ miles long. Although the railway picked up useful business when Millwall Football Club established its ground in the park, it was never particularly profitable. The inevitable closure came in 1926.

Millwall Viaduct, looking south towards North Greenwich.

Against all the odds, the viaduct survived, abandoned, for almost sixty years. Remarkably, a new lease of life came in 1987 with the building of the Docklands Light Railway. The station at Mudchute was more or less at ground level, but beyond that the light railway then utilised the old viaduct (which by now had been awarded listed status), by means of a connecting bridge to link it with the permanent way just south of the station. This was, however, only achieved at the cost of the line reverting from double track to single. The viaduct is too narrow for anything else.

The viaduct lived again – but not for long. The light railway was carrying record numbers of passengers, and there was an increasing demand for it to cross the river to serve south London. Accordingly, work commenced in early 1999 with the temporary closure of the line between Mudchute and Island Gardens (known in the days of the Millwall Extension Railway as North Greenwich). Island Gardens station had been built at the viaduct's far end; however, crossing the river by means of a tunnel entailed rebuilding the line below ground – thus rendering the old viaduct useless once more.

Shortly after the new, extended line under the Thames to Lewisham was opened, the bridge connecting Mudchute station to the viaduct was demolished, thus once again leaving it standing in isolation – awaiting, perhaps, a third lease of life in the future.

Millwall Park, being principally playing fields, is not the ideal place for artwork. Nevertheless, it does contain one important piece at its very southern end, though it is hard to see how a bronze statue of a woman caressing a huge fish has any relevance here. *Woman and Fish*, or rather this particular reproduction of it, is a prime part of the heritage of the London Borough of Tower Hamlets, in which the park lies. The original sculpture dated from about 1951 and was cast in concrete by the artist Frank Dobson. It stood in the north of the borough in Stepney and was used as a drinking fountain. However, successive attacks by vandals eventually damaged it beyond repair and it was removed in 2002. This reproduction was cast locally, in bronze, and was unveiled in 2007.

Island Gardens

Island Gardens is a short walk across Manchester Road at the southern end of Millwall Park (alternatively, DLR: Island Gardens). A small area of greenery on the tip of the Isle of Dogs, the gardens front the river and were opened in 1895.

From here, there are fine views of the Royal Naval Hospital or College and Queen's House across the Thames in Greenwich. The Hospital's architect, Sir Christopher Wren, more than three hundred years ago, proclaimed that what we now know as Island Gardens was the finest spot from which to appreciate it. This was an opinion presumably endorsed by the Venetian artist Antonio Canaletto when in 1755 he painted much the same view that we see today. It remains one of the classic paintings of London.

The classic view of Greenwich from Island Gardens, little changed since Canaletto's time. The Royal Naval Hospital frames Queen's House – which is actually set further back than this image suggests.

Island Gardens also mark the northern entrance to the Greenwich Foot Tunnel beneath the Thames. This was opened in 1902 as a substitute for the cross-river ferries that sailed from here and brought dockers from south London across the river to the Millwall and West India Docks. It remains one of the 'little adventures' of this part of the capital. Inside the domed entrance shaft, a lift transports pedestrians to the bottom of its 60-foot shaft. Alternatively, for the more energetic, a spiral staircase of eighty-eight steps serves the same purpose. (The author *has* counted them; and there are one hundred at the Greenwich end.) The tunnel, whose roof is a minimum of 13 feet beneath the riverbed, is 1,217 feet long and built of concrete-lined cast-iron rings. The footway is of York stone and 9 feet wide. However, upon walking through, it becomes apparent that it widens noticeably just beyond the Island Gardens end. This is a consequence of enemy action during the Second World War, when a bomb exploded on the riverbed, causing slight cracking. It was therefore reinforced from the inside, hence the difference in diameter. The walls throughout are lined with around 200,000 ceramic white tiles (which the author has not counted).

Thames Barrier Park

When the Thames Flood Barrier was completed in 1982, it would have been hard to imagine anything upstaging its steel wings that emerge gracefully from the river. However, eighteen years later and, in terms of aesthetically pleasing sights, it had a rival – Thames Barrier Park (DLR: Pontoon Dock).

Its 22 acres, on the eastern edge of Silvertown and overlooking the Thames Barrier, are on the site of a former petrochemical works. The site was heavily polluted – though no-one would know it now.

Its entrance is on the south side of North Woolwich Road, immediately adjacent to the light railway station. Initially, it seems almost minimalist in style, arriving visitors being greeted by a sunken paved area. However, the unwary soon discover that this houses an unusual water feature (unfortunately not always working), comprising thirty-two water jets that erupt at random intervals from ground level.

Visitors are not discouraged from walking through, or simply standing beneath them – a fine way of cooling off on a hot day.

The real eye-opener, however, lies just beyond. In effect, it is a huge trench sunk 13 feet into the surrounding landscape and stretching 450 yards – almost as far as the river. In an extremely clever way, it pays due deference to the heritage of the area – not least in that it almost resembles a dock; thus it is known as Green Dock. Nor is its planting style any accident: rows of clipped yew hedges shaped in the form of waves, and drifts of lavender maintain the watery theme among further formal clumps of planting. Festoons of trailing plants cloak the 'dock' walls, while footbridges criss-cross from side to side.

On either side of the 'dock' are less formal areas of grassland and wild-flower meadow, interspersed with drifts of young trees. Amid them all is a visitor centre and café, while at the riverside end of the 'dock' stands what appears to be an enormous shelter. It is, in fact,

The Green Dock at Barrier Park, looking north. Spiller's Millennium Mills are in the background.

a pavilion of remembrance to local people who lost their lives during two World Wars. The roof soars skywards; the sides are open to the elements. Inside, waves of black granite serve as impromptu seats for those seeking shade on a hot day. Beyond, a wooden decked area leads to a broad, riverside walk from where there are excellent views of the flood barrier.

Angular gravel paths defined by low-level polished granite walls lead from this area to the equally well-defined and angular Barrier Point development on the park's western periphery. Dating from 2000, this development of flats is built in a step-like fashion, culminating in a fifteen-storey curved block built on the riverside. Bright white throughout, its crisp lines more than complement the park.

Lyle Park

From Barrier Park, a ten-minute walk west along the main road, North Woolwich Road, leads to the older and altogether more traditional Lyle Park (DLR: West Silvertown). It is not especially large, being almost linear in form, nor especially easy to locate – almost as if this is one final secret that Docklands is unwilling to share. The entrance lies on Bradfield Road, a left turn off North Woolwich Road.

Lyle Park is still set in a predominantly industrial setting, and is built on land donated in 1924 by Abram Lyle & Sons, the syrup-making company whose successor still manufactures the product nearby (see the chapter on 'Britannia Village and Silvertown'). An initially narrow entrance adjacent to tennis courts soon widens out to an area about the size of a small football pitch. Beyond that, more formal rose gardens line a bank that forms the edge of a raised, riverside terrace – a peaceful spot to sit and watch the world pass by.

At the top of the steps leading to the terrace stand blue gates of intricate ironwork. They used to form the entrance to the former Harland & Wolff shipyard, located on Woolwich Manor Way at the entrance to the King George V Dock. The company first traded from the site in 1924 and specialised in smaller vessels and ship repair.

Lyle Park is little more than 100 yards across at its widest point, but it nevertheless contains tennis courts and a football pitch. This view looks north, away from the river.

The gates of the former Harland & Wolff shipyard at King George V Dock, re-erected in Lyle Park in 1994. A quiet riverside terrace is just beyond.

Although Harland & Wolff moved from that site in 1972, the gates were not re-erected in Lyle Park until 1994. The company's name is still displayed across their breadth, a reminder of the district's proud tradition and heritage.

East India Dock Nature Reserve

Old docks have been filled in, built over, boxed in and converted into marinas, so why should one not become a nature reserve? The theory has been put to the test at the former East India Dock entrance basin (DLR: East India), and it has worked extremely well.

With the closure of the East India Docks in 1967, the area soon fell into decay. It was almost twenty years before any attention was paid to it, and only in 1996 was work on the nature reserve completed. As such, it now forms the southernmost extremity of the Lea Valley Park.

There are three entrances, any of which is suitable for commencing a circular tour. For those visiting nearby Trinity Buoy

The former East India Docks entrance basin, now a nature reserve. The restored entrance lock is in the centre of the picture. A circuit of the entire reserve takes about ten minutes.

Wharf, there is an entrance on Orchard Place; alternative entrances are on Newport Avenue or off the Lower Lea Crossing. All are accessible by leaving the south side of East India station and walking east along Blackwall Way.

The entrance basin, and thus the nature reserve, is the only part of the East India Docks that remains in its entirety – although small areas have been filled in to create nesting areas for birds. Other than this, nature has been left to take its course: accordingly, parts of the reserve have started to silt up, resulting in the formation of saltwater marsh. (The basin is still fed by the tidal river.)

A huge variety of birds has been seen here, including cormorants, oystercatchers, Arctic terns and nightingales. Butterflies and dragonflies have also been drawn to the reserve, while wild flowers grow in abundance; buddleia has, almost inevitably, established itself on the quayside.

There are ample reminders of the basin's past – principally the two sets of lock gates connecting it to the Thames at its southern end. The lock gates were restored in 1997 – a fact proclaimed on their river-facing side. Considering that this lock was the sole means of entering the East India Docks, it becomes readily apparent how small, by today's standards, were the ships of earlier times.

It is possible to walk across the lock gates, thus enabling a complete circuit of the reserve to be made. This is also a good spot from which to view the original brickwork that lines the docks. Chains, presumably for mooring, still hang from the dock side, and mooring bollards are dotted throughout.

Jubilee Park, Canary Wharf

There is almost something oriental about Jubilee Park, Canary Wharf's principal green space, completed in 2002. Admittedly, it features neither pagodas nor the swathes of acers and colourful shrubs often associated with a Japanese garden, but there is something highly 'designed' about it.

A man-made stream runs its length, at waist level, along which there are more than twenty pools and fountains – although not of

Unlikely ever to open again, the restored lock gates of the East India Docks. This lock dates from 1897; the gates were made by the Thames Ironworks.

the kind that erupt high into the sky. Smartly trimmed hedges, and many of the hundreds of mature trees and thousands of shrubs that have been planted on the Canary Wharf Estate, add dimension. Among them are dozens of redwoods, which were up to 40 feet high when they arrived; what a sight they will make one day, against the adjacent tower – Number One, Canada Square. Bedding plants and spring bulbs add seasonal colour to the 2½-acre site, while its immaculately groomed lawns and generous supply of seats are extremely popular with office workers at lunchtimes in summer.

But perhaps the most incredible feature of Jubilee Park is what lies beneath it, for it is built on top of an underground car park, shopping mall and Canary Wharf Underground station. To all intents and purposes, then, this is a roof garden – at ground level.

Canada Square and Cabot Square, Canary Wharf

Canada Square Park is smaller and a little less formal than Jubilee Park. Mostly comprising well-maintained lawns and mature trees, it is better known for its blue flying saucer, an extremely popular piece of artwork. Installed in 1998 by Ron Arad Architects, this enormous glass-fibre structure is more properly known as *Big Blue* and is indeed all that we might envision a flying saucer to be as it seemingly hovers above the grass. As well as proving a delight to visitors, it also serves a more practical purpose – as a skylight to the underground shopping mall beneath.

Cabot Square is not a park at all – but a very pleasant and highly popular open space whose highlight is a central fountain. Low hedging, annual planting and a water feature comprising water cascading down a series of steps form part of the square's periphery.

BIBLIOGRAPHY AND FURTHER READING

Cherry, Bridget; O'Brien, Charles; Pevsner, Nikolaus. *The Buildings of England. London 5: East.* Yale University Press, 2005. Required reading, the definitive architectural guide to the area.

Conner, J. E. *Branch Lines of East London.* Middleton Press, 2000.

Conner, J. E. *Branch Lines around North Woolwich.* Middleton Press, 2001. Photographic guides to the area's railways.

Ellmers, Chris, and Werner, Alex. *Dockland Life.* Mainstream Publishing, 2000.

Ramsey, Winston G. (editor). *The East End, Then and Now.* After the Battle/Battle of Britain International Ltd, 2007.

Weinreb, Ben; Hibbert, Christopher; Keay, Julia; and Keay, John. *The London Encyclopaedia.* Macmillan, 2008.

Websites

There are many websites that cover various aspects of Docklands's history in great detail. The following are particularly recommended:

www.portcities.org.uk
www.british-history.ac.uk
www.royaldockstrust.org.uk

One of the largest and most thought-provoking pieces of Docklands artwork is at Prince Regent station, running along almost the entire boundary separating the adjacent bus station from the Beckton-bound platform. This stainless steel tableau by Brian Yale, made up of numerous panels, depicts the story of London's river and its docks from their earliest days, incorporating much of Docklands' social history and its people (including one panel featuring the artist's mother), together with its finest and grimmest hours. Anybody wishing to gain an understanding of the area could do worse than study it for half an hour or so.

Above: A potted history of Docklands at Prince Regent station. Here are four of the absorbing panels that make up the stainless steel frieze.

INDEX

Page numbers in italics refer to illustrations